MINNEAPOLIS
TRAVEL GUIDE 2024

Exploring the Hidden Gems and Sun-Soaked Splendor of Minneapolis in 2024

Ramiro Hassan

COPYRIGHT © 2024 BY RAMIRO HASSAN

TABLE OF CONTENTS

CHAPTER ONE: INTRODUCTION

Welcome to Minneapolis

Minnesota's biggest city, Minneapolis, is a bustling metropolis with a rich cultural, historical, and scenic legacy that is located along the Mississippi River. Known as the "City of Lakes," Minneapolis has a booming cultural scene, a strong economy, and a wide range of outdoor activities. The city is hospitable to all guests because of its progressive principles and diversified population. Minneapolis has plenty to offer everyone, whether they are history buffs, art lovers, foodies, or lovers of the outdoors.

A Synopsis of the Past

Since its beginnings as a mill town, Minneapolis has had a colorful history. The only natural waterfall on the Mississippi River, St. Anthony Falls, which supplied electricity for flour mills, is the focal point of the city. This industrial past is still evident today, especially along the riverside, where ancient mill ruins are conserved inside the Mill City Museum. By the late 19th century, Minneapolis had become the global center for flour milling, earning it the moniker "Mill City."

Climate and geography

Minneapolis and St. Paul, the adjacent state capital, are both included in the Twin Cities metropolitan region. The Mississippi River, many parks, and 13 lakes are just a few of the city's stunning natural environs. Minneapolis's weather is defined by chilly, snowy winters and hot, muggy summers. A wide range of year-round leisure pursuits are made possible by this variation in seasons, from boating and hiking in the summer to ice skating and skiing in the winter.

Customs and Society

Minneapolis is a center of culture with top-notch theaters, museums, and concert halls. The city's lively neighborhoods, each with a distinct personality, showcase the range of cultures present in the metropolis. There is a neighborhood to fit every interest, from the historic Mill District to the artistic North Loop.

Institutions like the Minneapolis Institute of Art, the Walker Art Center, and the Guthrie Theater are examples of the city's dedication to the arts. Minneapolis has a thriving music culture as well, having given birth to well-known performers like Bob Dylan and Prince. Every night of the week, live music is available in a variety of settings, from big concert halls to little bars.

Outside Activities

Minneapolis is an outdoor lover's dream come true. With a vast network of paths, lakes, and green areas, the city's park system is often rated as one of the finest in the country. Residents and tourists may swim, sail, paddleboard, cycle, and unwind at the Chain of Lakes, which includes Lake Calhoun (Bde Maka Ska), Lake Harriet, Lake of the Isles, Cedar Lake, and Brownie Lake.

Other recreational options along the Mississippi Riverfront include the picturesque Grand Rounds National Scenic Byway, which is a network of linked parks and parkways. Parks and lakes are transformed into wintry wonderlands throughout the winter, when people enjoy popular winter sports like ice skating, cross-country skiing, and ice fishing.

Hub of Education and Economy

Target, Best Buy, and the United States are just a few of the Fortune 500 corporations that call Minneapolis home. Bancorp. The city's economy is varied, including sectors that do well in technology, retail, healthcare, and finance. Large firms provide a vibrant business environment and draw in highly educated workers.

The city is renowned for its academic establishments as well. This is home to the University of Minnesota, one of the biggest public research institutions in the nation. The institution hosts a variety of public lectures, plays, and athletic events, which add to the city's lively intellectual and cultural life.

Accessibility and Transportation

An enormous transportation network connects Minneapolis to many locations. Easy access to both local and foreign locations is offered via the Minneapolis-Saint Paul International Airport (MSP). Without a vehicle, navigating the city is simple thanks to Metro Transit's public transit system, which consists of commuter trains, light rail, and buses. Minneapolis is one of the most bike-friendly cities in the country, with plenty of bike lanes and trails available for riders.

What's New in 2024

Minneapolis is still changing, and in 2024 there will be interesting new projects and developments that will draw more tourists and locals to the area. Here's what's new in Minneapolis this year, ranging from creative urban projects to cultural events and environmental efforts.

Infrastructure and urban development

1. Downtown East Commons extension: A major extension has taken place at the Downtown East Commons park, a prominent green area in the city. The project will create a lively community center for outdoor activities and events by adding additional recreational facilities, public art displays, and enhanced landscaping.

2. Revitalization of Nicollet Mall: The city's best area for eating and shopping has undergone a significant makeover. Expanded walkways, outdoor dining spaces, and improved lighting are just a few of the additional pedestrian-friendly amenities the project has added, making it an even more desirable destination for both residents and visitors.

3. North Loop Greenway: Known for its hip eateries and shops, the North Loop district now has a green space called the North Loop Greenway. This brand-new urban path encourages active transportation by connecting the area to downtown Minneapolis and offering bikes and pedestrians a beautiful route.

Highlights of Culture and Entertainment

1. Prince Museum Opening: A new museum honoring the life and work of the famous singer Prince has opened in downtown Minneapolis. The museum honors Prince's significant influence on music and culture with a wide range of artifacts, interactive displays, and concerts.

2. New sculptures by modern artists have been added to the Minneapolis Sculpture Garden, which is already a much-loved attraction. There are now more than sixty sculptures in the garden, including well-known works like "Spoonbridge and Cherry" by Claes Oldenburg as well as brand-new installations that showcase many creative viewpoints.

3. The Guthrie Theater, a mainstay of Minneapolis's cultural community, has revealed an intriguing schedule for its 2024 season. Highlights guarantee a vibrant and captivating experience for theatergoers, including world premieres of brand-new plays, beloved revivals, and partnerships with foreign theater groups.

Scene of Food and Drink

1. New Michelin-Star Restaurants: In 2024, a number of new eateries in Minneapolis will be awarded Michelin stars, demonstrating the city's thriving culinary industry. These restaurants, which are renowned for their creative food and top-notch service, have solidified the city's standing as a top dining destination.

2. Craft Brewery Boom: With numerous new breweries set to debut in 2024, the city's craft beer culture is expanding. Beer fans have a wide variety of alternatives to choose from at these breweries, which provide distinctive and regionally inspired beers ranging from standard lagers to experimental ales.

3. Improvements to the Minneapolis Farmers Market: The market has had a number of noteworthy improvements, such as the addition of more vendor spaces, better facilities, and a wider range of products. The market is currently a bustling and vital component of the city's culinary culture, with an increased number of local produce, artisanal items, and food booths.

Green initiatives and sustainability

1. Zero-Waste Initiative: Minneapolis has started a daring zero-waste program with the goal of raising recycling rates and drastically reducing trash by 2030. Increased public recycling bins, extended composting initiatives, and educational efforts to promote sustainable behaviors among locals and companies are all part of the plan.

2. Green Building Requirements: For all upcoming construction projects, the city has implemented new green building requirements. By giving priority to eco-friendly designs, sustainable materials, and energy efficiency, these criteria make sure that Minneapolis's expansion is ecologically responsible.

3. Urban Farming Projects: Minneapolis has launched a number of urban farming initiatives to support regional food production and green areas. These programs boost regional agriculture, provide chances for community gardening, and improve the urban environment of the city.

Well-being and health

1. New Wellness Centers: A number of brand-new holistic health facilities, including yoga, meditation, acupuncture, and wellness seminars, have opened in Minneapolis. Resources for inhabitants' physical and emotional well-being are offered by these facilities.

2. Increased Stations and Bike Availability: Minneapolis now boasts a larger network of stations for its bike-sharing program. The initiative offers an inexpensive, environmentally responsible method to learn about the city and promotes active transportation.

3. Healthy Living Campaigns: To encourage healthy living, Minneapolis has started a number of new public health initiatives. With the goal of boosting the community's general well-being, these programs include efforts to promote mental health, improve nutrition, and increase physical activity.

Innovation and technology

1. Smart City Initiatives: To enhance urban life, Minneapolis is adopting smart city technology. The city is becoming more sustainable and connected with new projects, including improved public Wi-Fi, energy-efficient street lighting, and intelligent traffic control systems.

2. Tech Startup Center: The city has created a brand-new center for tech startups that offers assistance and resources to up-and-coming tech firms. This center promotes innovation and entrepreneurship in Minneapolis by providing co-working spaces, networking opportunities, and mentoring programs.

3. Minneapolis is dedicated to creating new digital equality initiatives that will help close the digital gap. In order to enable all citizens to engage in the digital economy, these programs seek to provide underprivileged areas with inexpensive internet connections, training in digital literacy, and technological tools.

Social and community initiatives

1. Affordable Housing Initiatives: In response to the need for accessible housing, the city has started a number of new affordable housing initiatives. In order to build inclusive and sustainable communities, these initiatives will build new, affordable housing, renovate existing housing, and provide resident support services.

2. New youth empowerment initiatives have been launched in Minneapolis, offering young people access to mentoring, educational possibilities, and leisure activities. These initiatives are designed to help the young people in the city grow personally and professionally and set them up for success in the future.

3. Cultural Festivals and Events: With a variety of cultural festivals and events, the city keeps celebrating its varied population. New festivals that highlight the customs, artwork, and culinary traditions of many ethnic groups have been added for 2024 in an effort to promote harmony and understanding among locals.

Financial Progress

1. Minneapolis has innovation districts.

It was established new innovation districts in an effort to attract capital and advance economic growth. To promote development and the creation of jobs, these districts provide incentives to companies operating in important industries, including renewable energy, technology, and healthcare.

2. Workforce Development Programs: To provide citizens access to training and job possibilities, the city has increased the scope of its workforce development initiatives. These initiatives, which center on in-demand sectors and skill sets, facilitate economic mobility by bringing together employers and job seekers.

3. Minneapolis is dedicated to helping small companies by launching new programs that provide tools, money, and coaching. These initiatives seek to create an environment that is conducive to entrepreneurship so that small enterprises may prosper and boost the local economy.

Improvements in Transportation

1. Light Rail Expansion: By adding additional lines and expansions, the Minneapolis light rail system is growing and becoming more connected throughout the metropolitan region. By facilitating residents' and tourists' access to important locations, these extensions ease traffic congestion and advance environmentally friendly transportation.

2. Metro Transit has added environmentally friendly options to its public transportation system with the introduction of a new fleet of electric buses. These buses offer passengers a quieter, more comfortable ride while lowering emissions.

3. Pedestrian-Friendly Streets: In an effort to improve pedestrian safety, Minneapolis is putting new policies into place. These actions will make walking safer and more pleasurable by installing enhanced crosswalks, traffic-calming devices, and longer sidewalks.

Preservation of the Environment

1. Urban Reforestation: Thousands of trees have been planted across Minneapolis as part of the city's urban reforestation initiative. The objectives of this project are to beautify green areas, enhance air quality, and offer shade and beauty to locals and guests.

2. Enhancements to Water Quality: Minneapolis is funding initiatives to raise the standard of its rivers and lakes. In order to maintain the cleanliness and health of the city's waterways, these activities include stormwater management systems, pollution reduction measures, and habitat restoration.

3. New energy-efficiency initiatives have been launched by the city to assist citizens and companies in lowering their energy use. These initiatives stimulate the use of renewable energy sources, provide instructional materials, and give incentives for energy-saving improvements.

Education and the Arts

1. New Art Installations: Throughout the city, Minneapolis is getting more and more public art displays. These artworks, produced by regional and worldwide artists, improve the urban environment and provide locals and tourists with cultural enrichment.

2. Increased Educational Opportunities: To encourage lifelong learning, the city has launched new collaborations and educational initiatives. Assuring that locals of all ages have access to educational resources, these efforts include adult education courses, after-school programs, and partnerships with nearby colleges.

3. Community Arts Centers: New community arts centers in Minneapolis provide areas for teamwork and artistic expression. These facilities promote a thriving arts community and assist regional artists by providing seminars, concerts, and exhibits.

In summary

Minneapolis in 2024 will be a forward-thinking city that strikes a balance between history and progress, presenting a plethora of fresh projects and programs that improve the standard of living for both locals and tourists. The city is dedicated to building a vibrant, diverse, and forward-thinking community, and this is shown by everything from urban redevelopment initiatives and cultural extensions to environmental initiatives and technical advancements. There's something fresh and interesting to discover in Minneapolis this year, whether you want to take part in the city's zero-waste campaign, explore the new Prince Museum, or just enjoy the enlarged Sculpture Garden.

CHAPTER TWO: GETTING TO KNOW MINNEAPOLIS

History and Culture

The biggest city in Minnesota, Minneapolis, is known for its rapid expansion throughout the years, diversified population, and rich history and culture.

The Foundation and Early History

Dakota Sioux people lived in Minneapolis before European immigrants came in the early 1800s. The potential for water power in the region was highly valued, especially in the vicinity of St. Anthony Falls. Fort Snelling, built by the U.S. Army in 1819, drew inhabitants. The city was formally constituted in 1856 and merged with the municipality of St. Anthony in 1872.

Growth of the Economy

The early economy of Minneapolis was mostly reliant on the lumber and milling sectors, which used the Mississippi River's tallest cascade, St. Anthony Falls, to power flour mills. As the center of the world's flour milling during the late 19th century, Minneapolis gained the moniker "Mill City."

Cultural Evolution

As the city grew, immigrants from Eastern Europe, Germany, and Scandinavia were drawn to it, adding to its rich cultural diversity. Minneapolis's neighborhoods, each with its own cultural monuments and customs, are a testament to this variety.

Movement for Civil Rights

Minneapolis emerged as a prominent hub for the civil rights movement throughout the 1900s. Racial inequality and segregation were addressed in the 1960s and 1970s, mainly in the areas of housing and education. Additionally, the city was a major player in the labor movement, supporting equitable working standards and workers' rights.

Contemporary Minneapolis

Minneapolis is renowned today for its vibrant music and art sectors, thanks in part to well-known locals like Prince. The city is the center of the Midwest's cultural scene, with a large number of theaters, museums, and music venues. Notable cultural institutions include the Walker Art Center and the Minneapolis Institute of Art. Horace Cleveland, a landscape architect, created the city's park system, which is regarded as one of the finest in the country.

Weather and Best Times to Visit

An Overview of the Climate

Minneapolis has four distinct seasons and a humid continental climate. Warm summers, chilly winters, and comparatively mild springs and autumns define the climate.

Winter: December to February

Minneapolis experiences bitterly cold and snowy winters, with lows as low as -20°F (-29°C) and average highs frequently below freezing. There is a lot of snowfall in the city; on average, 54 inches (137 cm) fall there annually. January is usually the coldest month. Winter sports, including hockey, cross-country skiing, and ice skating, are popular despite the severe weather.

Springtime (April-May)

The average temperature rises gradually in the spring, from 34°F (1°C) in March to 65°F (18°C) in May. With sporadic snowstorms in the early part of the season and thunderstorms as the temperature rises, the season can be unpredictable. The many parks and gardens throughout the city are in full bloom in the spring.

August to June are summer months.

Summers are warm to hot, with July being the hottest month with average highs of 83°F (28°C). Thunderstorms are frequent, especially in the late afternoon and evening, and humidity can reach high levels. This is the main tourist season, suitable for outdoor activities like boating on the lakes, attending festivals, and touring the parks.

Autumn (September–November)

Autumn brings pleasant to chilly weather, with temperatures decreasing from an average high of 75°F (24°C) in September to 41°F (5°C) in November. The season is distinguished by magnificent autumn foliage, making it a pleasant time to visit. Early fall is also a fantastic period for outdoor activities before the approach of winter.

Ideal Times to Go

The activities you enjoy determine when is the best time to visit Minneapolis.

Summer (June to August): Ideal for outdoor activities, festivals, and enjoying the city's lakes and parks. Key events include the Minneapolis Aquatennial, a civic festival involving fireworks, parades, and more.

Autumn (September to October): Perfect for individuals who appreciate warm weather and beautiful hues. This season is less congested than summer, allowing a tranquil experience.

Snow (December to February): Great for snow sports enthusiasts. The city's parks and lakes provide ice skating, hockey, and skiing. However, prepare for really chilly weather.

Spring (March to May): Offers an opportunity to see the city in bloom and enjoy warmer weather. It's a calmer period for tourists compared to summer and winter.

Transportation Options

For both locals and tourists, Minneapolis has a wide range of transportation choices, making getting around the city and its environs simple.

Public Transport

The core of Minneapolis's public transportation network is the Metro Transit system, which includes light rail and buses.

Buses: Metro Transit runs a vast bus network that reaches every part of the city and its surrounding regions. Major bus lines operate every 10 to 15 minutes during peak hours. Bus routes are dependable and frequent.

Light Rail: The two main light rail lines are the Blue Line and the Green Line. From the Mall of America, the Blue Line travels through downtown Minneapolis and ends at Target Field. Via the University of Minnesota, the Green Line runs from downtown Minneapolis to downtown St. Paul.

Cycling The infrastructure in Minneapolis is well-known for being bike-friendly. With more than 200 miles of bike lanes and trails across the city, riding is a practical and well-liked form of transportation. Two notable trails are the Grand Rounds Scenic Byway and the 5.5-mile Midtown Greenway rail-trail route.

Vehicles and Ride-Sharing

Given the vast network of highways and roads in Minneapolis, driving is a popular form of transportation. Downtown parking might be difficult and pricey, but there are plenty of garages and lots accessible. For quick transport, many people utilize ridesharing services like Uber and Lyft, particularly for individuals who would rather not drive.

Scooters and shared bicycles

Scooter and bike sharing services, like Nice Ride, are available in Minneapolis and provide convenient, short-term rentals for exploring the city. The warmer months are when demand for these services is highest.

Strolling

Minneapolis's downtown is a great place to stroll about, and the Skyway systems that link the buildings provide indoor paths that are particularly helpful in the winter. There are many of eateries, retail establishments, and attractions close to one another.

Airport Access: The main airport servicing the Twin Cities is Minneapolis–Saint Paul International Airport (MSP). It's around ten miles south of Minneapolis's downtown and may be reached by bus, taxi, rideshare, and the Blue Line light rail. With a large number of internal and international flights, MSP is a significant hub.

Local Transit

There are several choices available for travel outside of Minneapolis:

Amtrak: Minneapolis is connected to Chicago, Seattle, and other major cities via the Amtrak Empire Builder route, which passes through the city.

Greyhound and Megabus: These bus companies provide reasonably priced long-distance transportation to a range of locations.

Car Rentals: There are several large car rental companies in the city that provide flexibility for local travel.

In summary

Minneapolis is a city that appeals to both locals and tourists with its rich history, varied culture, and abundance of transit options. Despite its fluctuations, the climate provides special chances for seasonal experiences and activities. Minneapolis has something to offer everyone, whether you're taking advantage of the effective public transportation system, exploring the arts scene, or just relaxing outside.

CHAPTER THREE: ICONIC LANDMARKS AND ATTRACTIONS

The Minneapolis Sculpture Garden

At 11 acres, the Minneapolis Sculpture Garden is one of the biggest urban sculpture gardens in the country, with over 40 pieces of modern and contemporary art. It's a 1988 partnership between the Minneapolis Park and Recreation Board and the Walker Art Center. The garden offers a smooth fusion of creative expression with the natural world, fostering a tranquil atmosphere for both residents and visitors.

Principal Draws:

1. Cherry and Spoonbridge: Built by Claes Oldenburg and Coosje van Bruggen, this famous artwork is a 51-foot-tall, over-7,000-pound giant spoon with a cherry on top. It is the focal point of the garden and a representation of Minneapolis.

2. Hahn/Cock: Sculpted by Katharina Fritsch, this artwork features a stunning blue rooster that rises about 25 feet tall and adds a quirky, fun touch to the landscape.

3. Arikidea: This dynamic sculpture by Mark di Suvero encourages participation as it sways in the wind. Its industrial construction contrasts sharply with the surrounding landscape.

4. LOVE: Robert Indiana's well-known LOVE sculpture, which has the word "love" in capital letters, is a favorite location for pictures and represents the global concept of love.

5. Standing Glass Fish: Located in the Alene Grossman Memorial Arbor and Flower Garden,

Frank Gehry's installation is a 22-foot-tall glass plate fish that symbolizes Gehry's often used fish theme.

Greenery & Gardens:

The sculptures are framed in color by a vivid array of seasonal flora found in the Alene Grossman Memorial Arbor and Flower Garden. With its collection of tropical and desert plants, the Cowles Conservatory provides a verdant, year-round green area.

Activities and Events:

The garden holds a number of annual events, such as seasonal festivals, educational seminars, and guided tours. Yoga in the Garden and other health pursuits draw those who want to become fit while learning about other cultures.

Amenities and accessibility:

The Minneapolis Sculpture Garden is free to the public and open every day from 6 a.m. to midnight.

Facilities include a nearby parking lot, bathrooms, and accessible walks.

The Walker Art Center

One of the most well-known modern art institutions in the country is the Walker Art Center, which is next to the Minneapolis Sculpture Garden. Since its founding in 1927, the Walker Art Center has developed into a globally renowned organization.

Exhibitions and Collections:

1. Permanent Collection: Over 13,000 items, including works by Andy Warhol, Jasper Johns, and Kara Walker, are part of The Walker's permanent collection. It encompasses a wide range of media, such as performing arts, film, video, painting, and sculpture.

2. Temporary Exhibitions: Both established and up-and-coming artists are regularly featured in the museum's temporary exhibitions. Merce Cunningham, Nairy Baghramian, and Julie Mehretu have all had recent exhibitions featuring their artwork.

3. Film and Video: The Walker's film and video program screens both classic and contemporary movies, frequently followed by talks with academics and filmmakers.

Design and Architecture:

The Walker Art Center's structure, created by Herzog & de Meuron, is a piece of art unto itself and opened its doors in 2005. The building stands out as a landmark in Minneapolis thanks to its unique aluminum mesh façade and angular design. The museum's interior features a number of connected galleries that make it easy to navigate between the many exhibitions.

Outreach and Instructional Initiatives:

A wide range of educational programs, including workshops, artist talks, and classes for all ages, are available at The Walker. The community can access contemporary art through events like Free First Saturdays and the Teen Art Council. Public tours and family-friendly events at the museum promote interaction with the artwork and a deeper comprehension of contemporary art.

Activities and Presentations:

Dance, theater, and musical performances are held at the Walker's McGuire Theater. Every year, the Out There series presents cutting-edge acts from all over the world. The Walker Art Center Gala and Rock the Garden, an outdoor music festival organized in association with Minnesota Public Radio, are among the special events held at the museum.

Accessibility and Visitor Information:

The Walker Art Center is open Tuesday through Sunday, with extended hours on Thursday evenings. Admission fees apply, but there are free admission days and discounts for students, seniors, and members. The center is fully accessible, with amenities including a restaurant, café, and gift shop. The underground parking garage offers easy access for guests.

The Guthrie Theater

The Guthrie Theater, founded in 1963 by Sir Tyrone Guthrie, is a cornerstone of Minneapolis's cultural scene. Known for its innovative productions and striking architecture, the Guthrie continues to push the boundaries of American theater.

Architecture:

The Guthrie's present building, built by Jean Nouvel and completed in 2006, is an architectural masterpiece. Its distinctive blue façade and cantilevered "Endless Bridge" overlooking the Mississippi River have made it a Minneapolis landmark. - Inside, the theater contains three performance spaces: the Wurtele Thrust Stage, the McGuire Proscenium Stage, and the Dowling Studio. Each provides a distinct theatrical experience, from tiny shows to huge performances.

Productions and Programming:

1. Classic and Contemporary Plays: The Guthrie is recognized for its high-quality presentations of both classic and modern plays. Its repertory includes works by Shakespeare, Chekhov, and Ibsen, as well as new pieces by current authors.

2. Musicals and New Works: The theater also presents musicals and new works, frequently partnering with writers, composers, and other theaters. Recent performances have featured "West Side Story" and the world debuts of new plays.

3. Community Engagement: The Guthrie's community engagement initiatives include seminars, courses, and conversations geared at nurturing a love of theater in people of all ages. Programs like "Guthrie Theater Lab" help local artists produce new work in a nurturing atmosphere.

Initiatives for Education:

A variety of educational activities are available at The Guthrie for adults, teachers, and kids. These consist of professional training programs for performers and theater professionals, summer camps, and student matinees. Students may interact with theater via internships, apprenticeships, and group projects thanks to the theater's partnerships with nearby colleges and institutions.

Activities and unique programs:

The Guthrie hosts a number of special events all year long, such as the Gala, which helps fund the artistic and educational endeavors of the theater.

The theatergoing experience is improved by audience engagement programs like backstage tours, post-show talks, and "Talk Backs" with the actors and crew.

Experience of Visitors:

In order to improve the experience of its guests, The Guthrie provides a number of amenities, such as the Sea Change restaurant, a gift shop, and breathtaking views of the Mississippi River from the Endless Bridge. With features like wheelchair seating, ASL-interpreted performances, and assistive listening devices, the theater is accessible to all guests.

In summary:

The Guthrie Theater, the Walker Art Center, and the Minneapolis Sculpture Garden are just a few of the city's well-known landmarks and attractions that each provide distinctive and enlightening experiences that demonstrate Minneapolis's dedication to the arts and culture. The Walker Art Center offers innovative contemporary art and provocative exhibitions; the Guthrie Theater presents top-notch theater in a breathtaking architectural setting; and the Sculpture Garden offers a serene yet dynamic outdoor art experience. Collectively, these establishments enhance Minneapolis's standing as a thriving center of the arts.

CHAPTER FOUR: HIDDEN GEMS OF MINNEAPOLIS

Secret Spots in Northeast Minneapolis

Known as "Nordeast," Northeast Minneapolis is a thriving and culturally diverse area of the city. Recognized for its unique atmosphere, creative community, and historic beauty, it has a few hidden gems that are well worth discovering.

1. Psycho Suzi's Motor Lounge: This eccentric tiki bar and restaurant is situated by the Mississippi River and is well-known for its whimsical decor and exotic concoctions. The multi-story building has a large terrace with breathtaking views of the river, as well as a number of themed suites. For those looking for a quirky and enjoyable dining experience, this is the ideal place.

2. The Sample Room: A hidden treasure for foodies, The Sample Room serves a changing selection of small plates produced with ingredients that are sourced locally. It's the perfect place for a relaxed evening with friends or a quiet dinner because of its small, cozy setting. The eatery also offers a carefully chosen assortment of wines and craft beers.

3. Betty Danger's Country Club: This out-of-the-ordinary country club has mini-golf, a Ferris wheel for dining, and a quirky vibe. Guests at Betty Danger's Country Club can savor inventive cocktails and Tex-Mex food while admiring one of the city's most spectacular views from the Ferris wheel.

4. Ard Godfrey House: The Ard Godfrey House, Minneapolis's oldest frame house still standing, provides a window into the city's pioneer history. Constructed in 1849, the house has been conserved as a museum offering guided tours that explore Minneapolis's prehistory and the lives of its pioneers.

5. Minneapolis Art District: The thriving arts district of Minneapolis is located in northeast Minneapolis. There are a lot of galleries, studios, and creative spaces in this area. The largest open studio tour in the United States, Art-A-Whirl, takes place every year and features the creations of hundreds of local artists. It's an event not to be missed. Year-round exploration of the neighborhood yields hidden treasures like the Northrup King Building, a former seed factory converted into an artist's haven.

6. Tattersall Distilling: Known for its creative cocktails and premium spirits, Tattersall Distilling is tucked away in an industrial area. Visitors can sample a range of products and learn about the distillation process by taking advantage of the distillery's tours and tastings. Its cocktail lounge is a chic and comfortable place to sip on a drink made by talented mixologists.

7. Casket Arts Building: Originally a casket factory, this historic structure is now home to innovative companies and artist studios. The Casket Artists Building is a nexus for the local artist community, hosting open studio activities and exhibits. It's a wonderful location to explore and find unique artwork and handcrafted things.

Quaint Neighborhood Cafes and Shops

Minneapolis is filled with quaint cafés and small stores that provide a more intimate and customized experience compared to bigger companies. Here are some outstanding spots:

1. Wilde Cafe & Spirits: Located in the historic Saint Anthony Main, Wilde Cafe & Spirits mixes old-world elegance with contemporary gastronomic pleasures. Named after Oscar Wilde, the café has Victorian-inspired décor and a menu that includes everything from breakfast staples to handcrafted drinks. It's an attractive setting for breakfast or an evening drink by the fireplace.

2. Five Watt Coffee: With many locations around Minneapolis, Five Watt Coffee is recognized for its revolutionary approach to coffee brewing. The Lyndale Avenue location, in particular, has a warm, eccentric ambiance and offers a unique menu of trademark cocktails like the Kingfield, which comprises espresso, coriander bitters, blackstrap molasses, and a splash of milk. The café also promotes local musicians, offering live concerts often.

3. Isles Bun & Coffee: Situated on the gorgeous Lake of the Isles, Isles Bun & Coffee is a celebrated bakery noted for its giant cinnamon buns, nicknamed "puppycakes." The quaint shop offers a variety of pastries, scones, and coffee drinks, making it a popular stop for locals and visitors alike.

4. Milkjam Creamery: This innovative ice cream shop, located in the Uptown neighborhood, offers unique flavors and dairy-free options. Milkjam Creamery is known for its creative concoctions such as Black (black coconut ash) and Cereal Killers (a mix of cereal milk ice cream and actual cereal bits). This sweet spot is even more appealing because of its lively and fashionable atmosphere.

5. Patina: With multiple locations throughout the city, Patina is a local favorite for gift shopping and offers a carefully curated selection of unique items at each location. Patina is a gold mine for those looking for unique finds, offering everything from quirky fashion accessories and home decor to locally made artisan goods. The store is a pleasant place to browse because of its cozy and welcoming atmosphere.

6. Spyhouse Coffee Roasters: Spyhouse Coffee Roasters has established itself as a mainstay in the Minneapolis coffee scene thanks to its chic interior design and expertly made coffee. Although every location has a unique personality, they are all dedicated to sustainability and high standards of quality. Specifically, the Northeast Minneapolis location offers a roomy, industrial-chic environment that's ideal for working or unwinding.

7. Hunt & Gather: This place is a must-see for fans of the vintage and antique. From quirky collectibles and oddities to retro decor and mid-century furniture, this eclectic store is brimming with treasures. Every visit is an adventure because of the whimsical displays and constantly changing inventory.

Uncharted Urban Parks

Minneapolis has a vast park system, but in addition to the well-known Chain of Lakes and Minnehaha Park, there are a number of lesser-known urban parks that provide peace and scenic views.

1. Boom Island Park: Located along the Mississippi River, Boom Island Park is a serene spot with scenic views of the downtown skyline. The park features a historic lighthouse, a riverfront trail, picnic areas, and boat docks. It's a great place for a leisurely walk, a bike ride, or simply to enjoy the peaceful riverfront ambiance.

2. North Mississippi Regional Park: Stretching along the west bank of the Mississippi River, this huge park provides a range of recreational options. The park features walking and bicycling paths, picnic spots, a nature-themed playground, and the Kroening Interpretive Center, which gives educational programs about the local ecology. The park's less-visited regions give a feeling of privacy and natural splendor.

3. Columbia Park: This big park in Northeast Minneapolis has a golf course, sports grounds, and picnic spots. The Columbia Park Pond, a serene area encircled by trees and walking paths, is one of its undiscovered treasures. The park also contains a disc golf course and a wading pool, making it a diverse venue for outdoor activities.

4. Theodore Wirth Regional Park: While Theodore Wirth Park is not entirely "hidden," its vast size means there are many lesser-known corners to explore. There are wetlands, open spaces, and trails surrounded by woods in the park. The Quaking Bog, a floating sphagnum moss bog, is a unique natural feature inside the park. The Eloise Butler Wildflower Garden, the oldest public wildflower garden in the U.S., is another hidden treasure inside the park, containing over 500 plant varieties and a calm, meditative ambiance.

5. Silverwood Park: Located just outside Minneapolis in St. Anthony, Silverwood Park is an arts and environmental learning center that combines natural beauty with creative expression. The park offers walking routes surrounding Silver Lake, outdoor art works, and a visitor center with gallery space and classrooms. It's a fantastic getaway for individuals seeking inspiration and calm.

6. Kenilworth Channel: This lovely canal links Lake of the Isles to Cedar Lake and is encircled by lush flora and calm pathways. The Kenilworth Channel is a serene hideaway inside the city, great for kayaking, canoeing, or just taking a leisurely walk along the water. Nature lovers will find the channel to be a hidden gem due to its remote atmosphere.

7. Father Hennepin Bluff Park: This park, which is on the east bank of the Mississippi River, provides breathtaking views of both downtown Minneapolis and the Stone Arch Bridge. The park's trails lead to picturesque overlooks as they wind through forested areas. It's a fantastic location for photography, birdwatching, or just taking in the riverfront scenery.

In summary

There are lots of undiscovered treasures in Minneapolis that are just waiting to be found. There's always something new to discover, whether it be in Northeast Minneapolis's diverse and artistic neighborhoods, charming local shops and cafes, or undiscovered urban parks. These lesser-known locations offer distinctive experiences that highlight the city's abundant natural beauty, vibrant culture, and strong sense of community.

CHAPTER FIVE: OUTDOOR ADVENTURES AND ACTIVITIES

Biking and Walking Trails

Minneapolis is known for having a vast network of excellent walking and bicycling paths, which makes it a haven for outdoor lovers. This extensive network of routes, which appeal to both casual walkers and serious bikers, is proof of the city's dedication to fostering a bike-friendly environment.

Grand Rounds Scenic Byway and Minnehaha Parkway:

Seven districts are connected by the 51-mile Grand Rounds Scenic Byway, which includes Minnehaha Parkway. Beautiful vistas of parks, lakes, and the Mississippi River may be seen from this walk. Popular routes include the more than 12-mile Minnehaha Parkway, which runs from Lake Harriet to Minnehaha Falls. The path offers lots of places for picnics and beautiful vistas, making it ideal for running, walking, and bicycling.

Regional Park of the Chain of Lakes:

Lake Harriet, Bde Maka Ska (formerly called Lake Calhoun), Lake of the Isles, and Cedar Lake are all part of the Chain of Lakes. There are designated bike and pedestrian trails all around each lake. With dedicated bike and pedestrian lanes, the trails around Bde Maka Ska and Lake Harriet are particularly well-liked. This helps to assure everyone's safety and pleasure. The paths are perfect for a leisurely stroll or an energizing bike ride because they are lined with trees, which provide shade and scenic beauty.

The Midtown Greenway

A 5.5-mile urban bike freeway that runs through the center of Minneapolis is called the Midtown Greenway. This old train corridor, which runs parallel to Lake Street, has been transformed into a bike and pedestrian path that provides a quick and secure way to get to work and play. The Greenway is accessible even in the winter because it is well lit and maintained all year round. Riders can reach the Chain of Lakes, different neighborhoods, and parks via a multitude of access points.

Park, Theodore Wirth:

Theodore Wirth Park, the Theodore Wirth Park, the largest regional park in the Minneapolis park system, has a vast network of hiking and biking trails. There are more than 12 miles of single-track single-track mountain bike trails in the park, suitable for riders of all skill levels. Apart from mountain biking, road cyclists and pedestrians can enjoy multiple paved trails. One of the highlights is the Quaking Bog Trail, which offers a distinctive stroll along a floating boardwalk within a five-acre bog.

Boom Island Park and Nicollet Island:

These parks, which are on the Mississippi River, are connected by a network of trails that provide breathtaking views of the downtown skyline and important historical sites. All ages and fitness levels can use the paths because they are fairly easy and flat. The Nicollet Island trail system offers views of the river and a peaceful environment with lots of greenery; Boom Island Park has picnic areas and a lighthouse.

Mississippi River Regional Trail:

This trail stretches along the Mississippi River, providing cyclists and walkers with breathtaking views of the waterway and its surrounding natural landscapes. The trail passes through several parks and historic sites, including the Stone Arch Bridge, a former railroad bridge that is now a pedestrian and bike path offering stunning views of St. Anthony Falls. This route is part of the broader

Mississippi National River and Recreation Area, which spans a 72-mile section of the river.

Bryant Avenue Bike Boulevard:

This north-south path offers a safe and calm alternative to larger streets, running parallel to main thoroughfares but with substantially less traffic. The boulevard is meant to emphasize cyclists, with traffic-calming measures in place to guarantee a safe and pleasurable ride. This path links numerous areas and gives access to different parks and services.

Cedar Lake Trail:

Known as America's first bike superhighway, the Cedar Lake Trail provides a straight and picturesque route from downtown Minneapolis to the western suburbs. The route is separated into distinct lanes for biking and walking, guaranteeing a safe and pleasurable experience for all users. Along the route, the path goes through stunning natural regions, including Cedar Lake and the Kenilworth Channel.

Mill District Trails:

Located in the historic Mill District, these paths provide a unique combination of urban and naturalnatural vistas. The region is rich in history, with the Mill City Museum and the Guthrie Theater situated nearby. The Father Hennepin Bluff Park and the Stone Arch Bridge, which give breathtaking views of the river and the cityscape of downtown, are accessible via the paths.

Lakes and Water Activities

The "City of Lakes," Minneapolis, is home to several lakes that provide a range of water-based recreational opportunities. These lakes are vital to the city's recreational environment, giving chances for swimming, boating, fishing, and more.

Bde Maka Ska:

Minneapolis's biggest lake, Bde Maka Ska, serves as a focal point for water sports. Numerous beaches around the lake,such as such as Thomas Beach and North Beach, are well-liked swimming locations. Boat rentals are also available at the lake for canoes, kayaks, paddleboards, and sailboats. The lake is home to species including walleye, northern pike, and largemouth bass, making fishing a popular pastime. The trail around the lake is great for cycling, running, and walking.

Lake Harriet:

A popular location for sailing and canoeing, Lake Harriet is renowned for its tranquil surroundings. Southeast Beach and North Beach, the lake's two public beaches, both provide safe and clean swimming places. A popular venue for live music and activities, the Lake Harriet Bandshell often draws audiences who enjoy the acts while having picnics by the lake. With so many different fish species to choose from, fishing is also quite popular here.

Nokomis Lake:

Another well-liked location is Lake Nokomis, particularly with families. Paddleboats and kayaks are among the many watercraft that can be rented at the lake, which also features a sizable beach area. The lake is often stocked with fish, making fishing a popular pastimepastime. In addition, Lake Nokomis is well-known for its picturesque bike and walking trails and for its lively community activities,such as such as the yearly Sandcastle Competition.

Cedar Lake:

Compared to the other lakes, Cedar Lake provides a more private and serene experience. There are three beaches on the lake, the most well-known being Hidden Beach. The lake's tranquil waters make it the perfect place for kayaking and paddleboarding.

Cedar Lake is an ideal location for bikers and joggers since it is linked to the Cedar Lake Trail.

The Lake of the Isles

Beautiful residences along the beaches of the Lake the Lake of the Isles, which is renowned for its scenic location. In addition to being a popular spot for kayaking and canoeing, the lake has a dog park for people who want to explore with their furry friends. The trails around the lake are ideal for taking a leisurely stroll or going for a bike ride since they provide beautiful views of the surrounding area and the water. The lake is a year-round recreational area since it is used for hockey and ice skating in the winter.

Minnehaha Creek:

Before draining into the Mississippi River, Minnehaha Creek passes past a number of lakes, including Lake Harriet and Minnehaha Falls. Kayaking and canoeing on the stream are quite popular activities, particularly in the spring and early summer when the water levels are higher. The stream is a beautiful place to paddle because of its gorgeous journey, which passes through several parks and natural regions. Along the stream, fishing is very popular, and there are a few nice sites to capture fish.

Lake Wirth:

Theodore Wirth Park is home to Wirth Lake, a well-liked swimming and fishing location. The lake is perfect for family vacations since it features picnic spaces and a sandy beach. Popular pastimes include canoeing and kayaking, with the lake providing a tranquil environment away from the bustle of the city. There are many hiking and bikingbiking routes in the nearby park, which expands the recreational options.

Mississippi River:

There are several different water sports available on the Mississippi River, such as paddleboarding, fishing, and boating. Boom Island Park and the Minneapolis Rowing Club are just two of the city's parks and boat launches that provide access to the river. Paddleboarding and kayaking are great inin the calmer areas of the river, and fishermen may catch species including walleye, catfish, and smallmouth bass. In addition, the river provides picturesque boat cruises that give a distinctive viewpoint of the city's natural beauty and famous sites.

Roberts Bird Sanctuary and the Rose Garden in Lyndale Park:

These nearby Lake Harriet attractions provide further outdoor adventures. The Rose Garden, which has hundreds of roses in a variety of hues and kinds, is a lovely place for a leisurely walk. With many pathways flowing through the woodland region and offering opportunitiesopportunities to witness a variety of bird species, Roberts Bird Sanctuary is a sanctuary for bird lovers.

Winter Sports and Ice Skating

During the winter, Minneapolis becomes a winter paradise,paradise, with plenty of ice skating and winter sports to choose from. With amenities and activities for people of all ages and abilities, the city's parks and lakes become centers of activity.

Ice Hockey:

There are a ton of artificial and natural ice skating rinks in Minneapolis, offering ice skating fans many alternatives.

The Ice Rink at the Depot:

One of the city's most well-liked indoor skating locations is the Depot Ice Rink, which is housed in a historic rail shed in the downtown area. With its quaint atmosphere and views of the city center, the rink provides a unique experience. It offers skate rentals and introductory training and is open from late November to early March.

The Lake of the Isles

Lake of the Isles becomes a sizable ice skating rink in the winter. The frozen lake is a flexible location for skaters of all sorts, including both hockey and pleasure skating rinks. The Minneapolis Park and Recreation Board looks after the rink, and it has warming rooms where skaters may stop and have some hot chocolate.

Chipotle WinterSkate:

Wells Fargo WinterSkate is a public outdoor rink that is free to use and is situated in Loring Park. The rink is a favorite hangout for families and recreational skaters, open from late November to February. There's a skate rental option and a festive mood thanks to the attractively adorned park around it with Christmas lights.

Bryant Square Park

Bryant Square Park has an outdoor ice rink that is kept cold and accessible all winter long. The park provides a warming hut for guests as well as skate rentals. The rink is a well-liked community space since it is used for both recreational skating and youth hockey.

Bde Maka Ska:

In the winter, Bde Maka Ska has a sizable natural ice rink with skate rentals and a warming shack. The frozen lake offers plenty of area for different ice sports, and the rink is well-liked for hockey and recreational skating. Snowshoeing and winter hikes are also possible in the nearby park area.

Winter Activities:

Skiing acrossthe country: the country:

There are many cross-country ski tracks in Minneapolis that are suitable for both traditional and skate skiing.

Park, Theodore Wirth:

Theodore Wirth Park has more than 15 miles of well-maintained cross-country skiing tracks, making it a popular destination for skiers. Both novice and expert skiers may enjoy the park,park, as it provides rentals and instruction. The paths provide a beautiful and demanding experience as they meander across open fields and lovely woodland regions. During the winter, the park also holds a number of skiing competitions and events.

Hiawatha Country Club:

The Hiawatha Golf Course is converted into a cross-country skiing venue for classic and skate skiing throughout the winter. It is appropriate for skiers of all skill levels because ofof the very flat terrain. The Minneapolis Park and Recreation Board looks after the course, so well-kept and easily accessible paths are guaranteed.

Park at Fort Snelling State:

There are more than 12 miles of well-maintained cross-country skiing trails at Fort Snelling State Park, which is close to the Mississippi and Minnesota River confluences. The park's picturesque paths provide a tranquil and breathtaking winter experience as they pass through grasslands, woodlands, and along riverbanks. In addition, the park features a warming house for guests and ski rentals.

Snowshoeing:

In Minneapolis, snowshoeing is a well-liked winter pastime, with several parks providing rentals and paths.

Minnehaha Park:

There are a number of snowshoe-friendly pathways in Minnehaha Park, which is also home to the well-known Minnehaha Falls. The frozen falls provide a spectacular background for a snowshoeing excursion, and the park's winter scenery is breathtaking. The park offers snowshoe rentals, which makes it simple for guests to explore the winter paths.

In Theodore Wirth Park, Quaking Bog:

Quaking Bog in Theodore Wirth Park provides a unique snowshoeing experience. The five-acre bog that the trail winds through offers a serene and isolated setting. The park is accessible to beginners and those interested in learning more about the natural history of the area because it provides guided tours and snowshoe rentals.

The Eloise Butler Bird Sanctuary and Wildflower Garden:

The trails in this sanctuary are great for snowshoeing in the winter. Snowshoeing through the sanctuary's wooded areas is a peaceful way to explore. The garden offers a different kind of beauty in the winter, with snow-covered trees and calm pathways, even though it is most famous for its flowers in the spring and summer.

Fishing on Ice:

In Minneapolis, ice fishing is a well-liked winter pastime, with several lakes providing fantastic angling conditions.

Lake Harriet:

A popular location for ice fishing is Lake Harriet, where enthusiasts pursue panfish, walleye, and northern pike. The lake is well-stocked, and rentable ice fishing huts provide warmth and cover for the duration of the fishing trip.

Cedar Lake:

Another well-liked spot for ice fishing is Cedar Lake, which is renowned for its tranquil environment. Northern pike, bluegill, and crappie may all be successfully caught in the lake. A typical activity for ice fishing aficionados is to construct their own transportable shelters and spend the day fishing on the frozen lake.

Nokomis Lake:

Lake Nokomis provides great ice fishing possibilities, with a variety of fish species accessible. The lake is constantly inspected for ice safety, and fishermen may rent ice fishing cabins to remain warm while fishing. The lake's closeness to residential areas makes it a suitable spot for local fishermen.

Winter Festivals and Events:

Minneapolis organizes various winter festivals and events that commemorate the season and provide extra outdoor activities.

The City of Lakes Loppet:

The City of Lakes Loppet is a significant winter festival hosted in Minneapolis, involving a variety of activities based on cross-country skiing. The festival features ski races, skijoring (when skiers are dragged by dogs), snowshoeing sports, and fat-tire bike races. The Loppet also incorporates a lantern loppet when players ski or walk around a track lighted by ice luminaries, providing a wonderful winter experience.

Holidazzle:

Every year, Loring Park hosts Holidazzle, a winter festival with a range of holiday-themed events and activities. Ice skating, light displays, a winter market, and live music are all part of the celebration. In addition, there will be sledding, heated houses, and food vendors selling winter fare during Holidazzle.

Winter Carnival in Minneapolis:

A long-standing custom that honors the winter season with a range of events and activities is the Minneapolis Winter Carnival.

CHAPTER SIX: DINING AND NIGHTLIFE

Must-Try Local Eateries

1. Spoon and Stable

Spoon and Stable, directed by Chef Gavin Kaysen, serves a New American cuisine that promotes fresh and locally sourced foods. Located in a converted stable, this café mixes rustic beauty with refined culinary choices. Dishes like the Minnesota-sourced duck and the braised beef short rib are highly recommended. The restaurant also includes a vibrant wine selection and artisan drinks that match the food nicely.

2. The Bachelor Farmer

The Bachelor Farmer, situated in the North Loop, specializes in Nordic-inspired food. Their menu, which varies periodically, comprises meals crafted from locally sourced ingredients. Must-try foods include their Swedish meatballs, roasted veggies, and the daily assortment of toasts. The nearby Marvel Bar, with its speakeasy ambiance, is great for a pre-dinner cocktail.

3. Alma Restaurant, helmed by Chef Alex Roberts, provides a three-course prix fixe menu that exhibits New American cuisine with worldwide influences. The restaurant, which also offers a café and a boutique hotel, stresses sustainability and farm-to-table principles. Standout meals include the house-made pastas and the grilled scallops.

4. Resurrection

Comfort cuisine and fried chicken are the restaurant's specialty at Revival, which has a Southern influence. Serving up substantial fare like Nashville hot chicken, shrimp and grits, and biscuits with honey butter, Revival has locations in Minneapolis and St. Paul. Both residents and tourists love it for its hearty tastes and laid-back vibe.

5. Adolescent Joni

James Beard Award-winning chef Ann Kim's Young Joni provides a distinctive fusion of American and Korean flavors. The wood-fired pizzas, such as the Korean BBQ and the Lady Zaza, are the restaurant's specialty. Not to be missed are their mini-meals, which include roasted cauliflower and kimchi. The appeal is increased by the speakeasy-style rear bar that serves creative drinks.

6. Hai offers Northeast Minneapolis the bright tastes of Southeast Asia. Chef Christina Nguyen created the menu, which includes items like pho, turmeric dill fish, and crispy rice salad. For those looking for robust and genuine tastes, this restaurant is a must-visit because of its vivid atmosphere and tropical drinks, which elevate the eating experience.

7. A Martina

Martina incorporates both Italian and Argentinean characteristics. Fresh seafood, handcrafted pastas, and wood-grilled meats are some of the dishes on Chef Daniel del Prado's menu. Duck confit and octopus a la plancha are two of the restaurant's signature dishes. Popular eating location because of its creative cocktail program and beautiful atmosphere.

8. Brasa Rotisserie Premium

Chef Alex Roberts, a James Beard Award winner, founded Brasa Premium Rotisserie, which serves comfort cuisine with a Caribbean and Latin flair. They serve slow-roasted meats such as rotisserie chicken and pork, with sides like collard greens and yuca fries. The relaxed ambiance and emphasis on regional foods distinguish Brasa.

9. Tilia is a well-liked local cafe situated in the Linden Hills district. A range of American cuisine with an emphasis on seasonal, fresh ingredients is offered on the menu. The pappardelle with rabbit, the house-made sausage, and the fish taco torta are all popular dishes. It's the ideal location for a leisurely dinner because of the cozy, welcoming ambiance.

10. Grassa Bar Pasta lovers will appreciate La Grassa in the North Loop. Chef Isaac Becker created the menu, which has a wide variety of homemade pasta dishes such as crab ravioli and gnocchi with orange and cauliflower. It's popular for both formal events and casual get-togethers because of the lively atmosphere and extensive wine selection.

Craft Breweries and Distilleries

1. Brewery Surly Co.

One of the most well-known breweries in Minneapolis is Surly Brewing Co. Situated in Prospect Park, Surly has an extensive selection of specialty beers, ranging from deep stouts to zesty IPAs. Enjoying their signature Furious IPA or seasonal offerings in a beautiful atmosphere is made possible by their huge beer hall and outside beer garden. In addition, Surly's kitchen offers a selection of pub cuisine, such as sandwiches and pizzas.

2. Brewing Company, Indeed

The Northeast Arts District's Indeed Brewing Company is well-known for its creative and superior brews. Try beers like the Mexican Honey Imperial Lager and Day Tripper Pale Ale in their well-liked taproom. Indeed is renowned for its commitment to the community, regular food trucks, and event hosting.

3. Brewery Fulton

Nestled in the North Loop, Fulton Brewery is a trailblazer in Minneapolis's craft beer culture. The Sweet Child of Vine IPA and the Lonely Blonde are just two of the beers available in their lively taproom. Fulton also maintains a food truck on-site, selling burgers, sandwiches, and other delectable nibbles.

4. Brewing Company Modist.

Modist Brewing Co. is notable for its innovative brewing methods. They stretch the limits of conventional brewing methods with their inventive brews, such as the First Call coffee lager and the Dreamyard hazy IPA. The North Loop Taproom provides a contemporary, industrial atmosphere in which to savor their distinctive offerings.

5. Brewery Dangerous Man Inc.

Located in the Sheridan district, Dangerous Man Brewing Co. is a well-known small-batch brewery. Well-known for their assortment of inventive and tasty beers, their best-selling selections include the Chocolate Milk Stout and the Peanut Butter Porter. To taste their wide selection of beers, stop by the comfortable taproom.

6. Distillation Tattersall

Among the spirits produced by Tattersall Distilling, which is situated in Northeast Minneapolis, are liqueurs, vodka, and gin. They have a chic cocktail area where customers can savor well-mixed drinks created with their own spirits. Eastside Gin & Tonic and Tattersall Old Fashioned are two popular beverages.

7. The Distillery Norseman

Located in northeast Minneapolis, Norseman Distillery is well-known for its inventive cocktails and handcrafted spirits. Among the spirits produced at their distillery are vodka, gin, rum, and whiskey. To savor their creative concoctions, including the Beet Negroni and Smoked Pear, in a unique and cozy atmosphere, go to the cocktail area.

8. Brew Labs at Bauhaus

Inspired by the Bauhaus school of design, Bauhaus Brew Labs brews tasty and vivid beers. Brews like Wonderstuff Pilsner and Sky-Five! IPA are popular at Bauhaus, a popular venue to sip beer located in the Northeast Arts District. The brewery serves as a nexus for the community by often hosting events and food trucks.

9. Cooperative Fair State Brewing

The goal of the member-owned Fair State Brewing Cooperative is to provide a broad range of excellent beers. Fair State Brewery, situated in northeast Minneapolis, is renowned for its creative and cooperative brewing methods. Two of their signature beers are the Pils and the Roselle, a sour lager laced with hibiscus.

10. Cider Werks Social

Sociable Cider Werks' selection of artisan ciders provides a delightful substitute for conventional beer. The friendly Sociable taproom in Northeast Minneapolis is a great place to try their signature beers, including the Freewheeler and Spoke Wrench. They also make seasonal specialties and a range of fruit-infused ciders.

Best Bars and Nightclubs

1. Jazz Club Dakota

A well-known location that offers top-notch food along with live music is the Dakota Jazz Club. The Dakota, a downtown Minneapolis venue, presents jazz performers from throughout the country. It's a popular destination for music enthusiasts because of the cozy atmosphere and excellent acoustics. With a variety of American foods on the menu, it's the ideal spot for supper and entertainment.

2. First Avenue

First Avenue is a legendary concert hall that has a significant place in Minneapolis music history, especially with Prince. Live artists ranging from worldwide acts to local bands play in the main room and the 7th Street entrance. The iconic prominence of the theater is further enhanced by its black facade, which is covered with stars with the names of artists.

3. The Ice House

Icehouse is a multipurpose space that functions as a restaurant, music club, and bar. The varied live music program at Icehouse, which is situated in the Whittier area, includes jazz, indie, and techno performers. A variety of inventive American cuisines are available on the menu, while handmade cocktails and regional beers are served at the bar.

4. Marvel Bar

Tucked down under The Bachelor Farmer, Marvel Bar is a speakeasy-style cocktail bar renowned for its creative concoctions and welcoming atmosphere. The bartenders utilize premium alcohol and homemade ingredients to create inventive drinks. Cocktail aficionados love it because of the cozy atmosphere and careful attention to detail.

5. Bar Room at Tattersall Distilling

Using Tattersall's own spirits, professionally created cocktails are served to guests in the chic Tattersall Distilling Cocktail Room. A variety of traditional and creative concoctions, showcasing the distillery's liqueurs, vodka, and gin, are offered on the cocktail menu. The stylish, industrial environment enhances the allure.

6. The Bar of Prohibition

Situated on the 27th story of the Foshay Tower, Prohibition Bar provides breathtaking views of Minneapolis's downtown area. The bar offers a selection of specialty cocktails and premium wines, and its elegant décor dates back to the 1920s. It's the ideal location for a great night out because of the sophisticated surroundings and skyline views.

7. The Pourhouse

Within the Lumber Exchange Building is a vibrant bar and nightclub called

The Pourhouse.

The Pourhouse is well-known for its vibrant ambiance and wide drink selection. It also offers a large dance floor, themed events, and live DJs. It's a well-liked spot for those who like to dance and take in the exciting nightlife.

8. Downtown Minneapolis

Up-Down Minneapolis is a bar and a retro arcade combined. Up-Down, a Lyn-Lake establishment, offers more than fifty arcade games from the 1980s and 1990s, along with a large assortment of craft beers and specialty drinks. There is more seating and fantastic city views on the rooftop terrace.

9. The Gay Nineties

Gay 90s is a legendary LGBTQ+ club located in Minneapolis's downtown. The multi-story club has many dance floors with different musical genres, such as pop, hip-hop, drag, and karaoke. It is an important part of the city's nightlife because of its lively and inclusive environment.

10. The Irish Pub Kieran's

In the heart of Minneapolis, Kieran's Irish Bar provides a classic Irish bar atmosphere. The pub offers traditional Irish cuisine and beverages, live music, and quiz evenings. It's a well-liked meeting place because of the cozy, welcoming ambiance and regular activities.

11. Palmer's Bar

Palmer's Bar is a dive bar with a long history that is located in the Cedar-Riverside district. Palmer's, which is well-known for its eclectic crowd and unpretentious feel, has live music, inexpensive beverages, and a laid-back environment. Both residents and tourists like this cherished establishment.

12. The Neighborhood

The Local is an Irish bar in the middle of downtown Minneapolis that serves substantial pub food and a wide assortment of whiskeys. An inviting atmosphere is created by the staff's friendliness and the interior's warm wood paneling. Try the famed whiskey sour and the fish and chips from The Local.

13. Volstead's Emporium

Lyn Lake is home to a secret speakeasy called Volstead's Emporium. With a secret code and an unmarked entrance, the pub provides a cozy atmosphere and well-made beverages. It's a unique nightlife experience, with its inventive beverages and design inspired by the Prohibition period.

14. The Armory

Once a historic location, The Armory is now a top live music and event facility. The Armory, a downtown venue, accommodates big events and a variety of music, including rock and EDM. The modern sound system and striking building add to the whole experience.

15. The Polonaise Room at Nye

A treasured Minneapolis landmark, Nye's Polonaise Room is well-known for its piano bar and vintage dinner club atmosphere. Nye's, a Polish-American restaurant in Northeast Minneapolis, serves a variety of substantial cuisine and has live piano music. It is a distinctive and unforgettable location because of the colorful ambiance and quirky furnishings.

In summary

Minneapolis has a lively, diversified food and entertainment scene. The city offers something for every palette, from must-try local restaurants serving creative and savory food to artisan brewers and distilleries creating premium beers and spirits. With a variety of pubs and nightclubs to suit all interests and inclinations, the nightlife is equally spectacular. Minneapolis provides a wide range of activities that capture its vibrant and inviting atmosphere, whether you're searching for an elegant cocktail bar, an exciting concert venue, or a vintage arcade.

CHAPTER SEVEN: ARTS AND ENTERTAINMENT

The Minneapolis Music Scene

Background Information in History

The rich musical history of Minneapolis has had a big impact on American music. The city is well known for having influenced the growth of several musical genres, most notably alternative, rock, and funk. Legendary musician Prince invented the Minneapolis Sound in the late 1970s and early 1980s. It is a blend of funk, rock, pop, and new wave. His impact helped establish Minneapolis as a significant music destination, along with that of groups like The Replacements and Hüsker Dü.

Principal Locations: First Avenue and 7th St. Entry: This legendary location, often connected to Prince's "Purple Rain," has been a mainstay of the

Minneapolis music landscape since 1970. It presents a wide range of live events, from globally recognized performers to small-town independent bands.

The Cedar Cultural Center: This nonprofit organization, well-known for its eclectic schedule, hosts international music events to foster an understanding of diversity across cultures.

The Dakota Jazz Club: This location presents jazz, blues, and soul music in a cozy atmosphere. Renowned performers, including Wynton Marsalis and Norah Jones, have performed there.

The Armory is a bigger location that holds significant events and concerts. Renowned for its exceptional acoustics, Post Malone and Metallica have performed there.

Local performers and bands

Hippo Campus is a St. Paul indie rock group that has become well-known around the country for their upbeat live shows and appealing tunes.

Dessa: A prominent figure in the Minneapolis music scene, Dessa is a rapper, singer, and lyricist who is a member of the Doomtree collective.

Soul Asylum: This alternative rock group, well-known for the classic song "Runaway Train," has been a mainstay of the Minneapolis music scene since the 1980s.

Radio Stations and Media: Minnesota Public Radio's The Current (89.3 FM) is a major supporter of alternative music both locally and nationally. It regularly presents live in-studio shows and gives assistance to up-and-coming musicians.

Radio K (KUOM): Run by the University of Minnesota, this station provides a wide range of musical genres and serves as a vital venue for regional musicians.

Music Festivals: Basilica Block Party: A combination of local and national musicians perform throughout this annual summer event.

The purpose of the event is to gather money for the Basilica of Saint Mary's repair.

Twin Cities Jazz Festival: This free event in St. Paul attracts jazz fans from all around the area to see performances by regional and foreign performers.

Local Art Galleries and Studios

Important Art Galleries: Walker Art Center: Among the most well-known modern art museums in the US, the Walker Art Center has a sizable collection of modern and contemporary art, including pieces by Chuck Close and Edward Hopper. The famous "Spoonbridge and Cherry" sculpture is located in the Minneapolis Sculpture Garden, which is close to it.

MIA, the Minneapolis Institute of Art: MIA is well-known for its extensive collection, which includes approximately 90,000 pieces of art covering 5,000 years of history. Asian art, modern items, and works by European masters are among the highlights.

The Weisman Art Museum, which is housed on the University of Minnesota campus, is well-known for both its collection of contemporary art and its distinctive Frank Gehry-designed structure.

Prestigious art collectives and studios

Northrup King Building: Originally a seed business warehouse, this space now houses over 300 galleries and artist studios. It serves as the Northeast Minneapolis Arts District's central point.

Casket Arts Building: Another important site in the Northeast Arts District, this building is home to a varied community of creatives and artists. It often has exhibits and open studio times.

Highpoint Printmaking Center: Highpoint is a nonprofit studio that provides space for printmakers and organizes educational events and exhibits.

First Thursdays in the Arts District: Several studios in the Northeast Arts District open their doors to the public on the first Thursday of every month, providing a close-up look at the creations and methods of the artists. These events include art walks and open studios.

Art-A-Whirl: Held in Northeast Minneapolis each year, Art-A-Whirl is the biggest open studio tour in the United States, showcasing hundreds of artists working in a variety of media. In addition to seeing live demonstrations, visitors may buy artwork directly from artists.

Murals and public art

Midtown Greenway Murals: The many murals that cover this urban path pay homage to the rich cultural diversity and rich histories of the districts it travels through.

Powderhorn Park Murals: Powderhorn Park is well-known for its colorful murals, many of which are the result of neighborhood initiatives that highlight local pride and social concerns.

Community Programs and Art Education

Juxtaposition Arts: A youth-oriented visual arts facility that offers possibilities for young artists to grow professionally and get instruction. Through art, it seeks to promote creativity and community involvement.

Minnesota Center for Book Arts: This facility offers access to a variety of printing and binding processes, instructional events, and exhibits to support the book arts.

Festivals and Events in 2024

Winter and Spring activities: Ice sculpture, winter bicycling, and outdoor concerts are just a few of the activities that take place during the Great Northern Festival, which runs from January 25 to February 4. This festival offers a range of cultural and outdoor events to encourage people to enjoy the winter season.

Art Shanty Projects (January 20 - February 11): Held on a frozen lake, this unique event comprises artist-created shanties and performances, converting the winter landscape into a participatory art setting.

January 27th, Lake Harriet Winter Kite Festival: A brilliant show of kites soaring over Lake Harriet, accompanied by marshmallow toasting, ice fishing, and horse-drawn wagon excursions.

Summer Events: Northern Spark (June 8–9) is an all-night arts event that uses interactive exhibitions, performances, and art installations to change public locations across Minneapolis. The annual topic promotes contemplation on environmental and societal concerns.

Twin Cities Pride Festival (June 22–23): One of the Midwest's biggest LGBTQ+ pride festivals, including a parade, drag performances, live music, and community activities held at Loring Park.

State Fair of Minnesota (August 22–September 2): The fair has notable art contests, exhibits, and live music events, yet it is not only an arts festival. It's a significant cultural event and one of the biggest state fairs in the United States.

Fall Events: Minnesota Renaissance Festival (Weekends, August 17–September 29): This annual festival, which takes place in Shakopee, close to Minneapolis, has been around for a long time and features jousting, craftspeople, and entertainment from that era.

Twin Cities Film Fest (October 16–26): This festival, which presents independent films, brings together audiences and filmmakers for special events, panel discussions, and screenings.

Monthly and Continual Events

Minnesota Orchestra Season: A comprehensive program of classical concerts, including partnerships with modern artists and thematic performances, is provided by the Minnesota Orchestra. Orchestra Hall, where they reside, is renowned for having superb acoustics.

Guthrie Theater Season: Plays from both the classic and modern repertory will entice spectators to the Guthrie Theater's magnificent three-stage complex with a view of the Mississippi River in 2024.

North Loop Gallery Crawl (First Fridays): This monthly gathering allows people to explore contemporary art exhibits and interact with artists at galleries in the North Loop district until late.

Special Exhibitions and Events in 2024: "Art Expanded, 1958-1978," a major exhibition organized by the Walker Art Center, will take place from March 3 to June 23, 2024. It will examine the creative explosion that occurred during a pivotal moment in the history of contemporary art.

"Rembrandt and His Circle," an exhibition at the Minnesota Institute of Art, which runs from April 12 to August 18. It highlights Rembrandt's output and how he influenced pupils and other artists.

"Global Art Local" at the Weisman Art Museum (February 14–May 12): This exhibition will address topics of migration, identity, and cultural interaction while showcasing the work of foreign artists who call Minnesota home.

Festivals of Community and Culture

MayDay Parade and Festival (May 5): This yearly celebration in Powderhorn Park celebrates spring with big puppets, live music, and community performances. It is organized by In the Heart of the Beast Puppet and Mask Theatre.

Holidazzle (November–December): An annual celebration in Loring Park with lights, fireworks, a winter market, and live performances by neighborhood artists.

Stone Arch Bridge Festival (June 15–16): Live music, visual arts, and family-friendly events are all part of this summertime celebration situated beside the iconic Stone Arch Bridge.

Other Prominent Occasions: Open Streets Minneapolis: During the summer, a number of municipal streets are made inaccessible to cars in favor of bicycles, pedestrians, and community events. It's an occasion to celebrate community involvement and active transportation.

August 1–11, Minnesota Fringe Festival: The Fringe Festival provides a space for independent and experimental theater, dance, and performance art, showcasing hundreds of shows in various locations across the city.

From its rich history of important music and a thriving gallery scene to its many festivals and cultural events, Minneapolis's lively arts and entertainment industry is distinguished by its diversity of offers. The city offers both locals and tourists a wide variety of year-round events that demonstrate its dedication to innovation and community involvement.

CHAPTER EIGHT: FAMILY-FRIENDLY ACTIVITIES

Kid-Friendly Museums and Attractions

1. The Children's Museum of Minnesota

Address: 10 7th St. W., St. Paul, Minnesota 55102

Features: interactive displays designed for kids, creative laboratories, and hands-on exhibitions. For toddlers, popular exhibitions include "Sprouts," "The Scramble," and "Forces at Play."

Special programs include birthday celebrations, sensory-friendly playdates, and family nights.

2. Minneapolis Science Museum

120 W Kellogg Blvd., St. Paul, MN 55102 is the address.

Features: interactive displays with an emphasis on technology, physical science, and natural history.

The Mississippi River Visitor Center, the Experiment Gallery, and the Dinosaurs & Fossils Gallery are among the highlights.

Special Programs: Camp-ins, OmniTheater, and unique exhibits delving into the history of video games, such as "Game Changers."

3. History Center of Minnesota

Address: 345 W Kellogg Blvd., 55102 St. Paul, MN

Features: Children-only exhibit "Then Now Wow," one of many interactive displays examining Minnesota's past.

Special Programs: Craft classes, family days, and live history shows.

4. The Museum of Bakken

3537 Zenith Ave. S., Minneapolis, MN 55416 is the address.

Features: interactive exhibitions that highlight electricity and magnetism. For kids, "Spark of Life" and "Ben Franklin's Electricity Party" are very entertaining.

Special programs include family science evenings, STEM-focused events, and summer camps.

5. The Bell Museum

Address: 2088 Larpenteur Ave. W., 55113 St. Paul, MN

Features: touch-and-see laboratories, animal dioramas, and a planetarium are all part of this natural history museum.

Special Programs: Seasonal seminars, outdoor excursions, and star parties.

Parks and Playgrounds

1. The Regional Park of Minnesota

Highlights: 193 acres of parks with playgrounds, picnic spots, a wading pool, and a breathtaking 53-foot waterfall.

Activities: summertime live music at the bandshell, hiking trails, biking, and disc golf.

2. Regional Park Theodore Wirth

Features: lakes, gardens, and pathways spanning more than 740 acres. The Quaking Bog and the Eloise Butler Wildflower Garden and Bird Sanctuary are part of it.

Activities include tubing, skiing, snowboarding, hiking, mountain biking, and a sizable playground.

3. Reserve for Hyland Lake Park

Features: The expansive, creative Hyland Play Area, often called "Chutes and Ladders," is a playground.

Activities: boating, fishing, hiking, bicycling, and cross-country skiing in the winter.

4. The Park at Lake Harriet

Features: Plenty of walking and bicycling routes around the lake; a rose garden; a bird sanctuary; and a bandshell.

Activities: going to movies or concerts in the park, fishing, boating, and picnics.

5. Park Gardens at Lyndale Park

Features: The Rose Garden, Perennial Garden, and Peace Garden are just a few of the themed gardens.

Activities: strolling around the gardens, seeing birds, and hiking.

6. Park of Mill Ruins

Attractions: Historic flour mill ruins and educational exhibits may be seen here, which is situated by the Mississippi River.

Activities: biking along the riverbank, historical discovery, and walking tours.

Seasonal Activities for Families

1. Summer Activities: Aquatennial Festival: This July celebration features sandcastle competitions, parades, fireworks, and racing in milk carton boats.

"Twin Cities Pride Festival": Held in Loring Park, this family-friendly celebration of LGBTQ+ pride features entertainment and activities.

Minneapolis Sculpture Garden: Great for strolls and picnics in the summer, this outdoor art installation features the famous "Spoonbridge and Cherry."

2. Fall Activities: Shakopee's "Sever's Fall Festival and Corn Maze" has a huge corn maze, a petting zoo, enormous slides, and a pumpkin patch.

Jack-O-Lantern Spectacular at the Minnesota Zoo: A strolling route lined with thousands of carved pumpkins lit up.

Apple Picking: Hayrides, corn mazes, and apple picking are available at nearby orchards, including Afton Apple Orchard and Minnetonka Orchard.

3. Winter Activities: Holidazzle: An event celebrating winter in Loring Park, including ice skating, seasonal markets, live music, and Christmas lights.

Wells Fargo WinterSkate: Rice Park in downtown St. Paul is home to an outdoor ice skating rink that is free to use with skate rentals.

Ice Castles: These castles, which are near New Brighton, include slides, tunnels, and sculptures that are constructed completely of ice.

4. Spring Activities: Minnesota Landscape Arboretum: Gorgeous springtime scenery, cherry blossoms, and family-friendly hiking routes.

Maple Syrup Festival at Gale Woods Farm: Farm tours, tastings, and demonstrations of tapping maple syrup.

Farm Babies at the Minnesota Zoo: A springtime celebration featuring newborn animals, such as lambs, calves, piglets, and chicks.

Final Thoughts

There are plenty of family-friendly activities in Minneapolis that are appropriate for every season. Families have many options to explore, learn, and spend quality time together, from interactive museums and captivating parks to distinctive seasonal events.

CHAPTER NINE: SHOPPING IN MINNEAPOLIS

Unique Boutiques and Local Shops

Cliché

Uptown-based Cliché provides a stylish assortment of women's apparel and accessories. The store is well-known for its distinctive items made by regional designers as well as its tailored shopping experience.

MartinPatrick3

MartinPatrick3, a renowned men's store in the North Loop, offers a high-end shopping experience with an extensive selection of apparel, housewares, and accessories. The business places a strong emphasis on superior customer service and high-quality merchandise.

Parc Boutique

Parc Boutique is a modern women's apparel and lifestyle store located on the North Loop. Simple but elegant apparel, jewelry, and home décor items are all part of the carefully chosen collection.

Home Goods The Foundry

The Foundry Home Goods is popular for distinctive domestic goods and minimalist home décor in the North Loop. The store specializes in well-made, useful items that are both elegant and useful.

Mille

Mille is a South Minneapolis store that sells home products, accessories, and clothes for women. Reputable for its well-chosen assortment of independent designers' creations, the store exudes style and ease.

Popular Shopping Districts

Uptown

Uptown Minneapolis is a vibrant neighborhood that is home to a variety of hip shops, national chains, and distinctive restaurants. Calhoun Square and Hennepin Avenue, which are dotted with stores, cafés, and entertainment venues, are noteworthy locations.

North Loop

The Warehouse District, also referred to as the North Loop, has evolved into a bustling retail area. It provides a variety of upscale boutiques, antique stores, and home goods retailers. MartinPatrick, Grethen House, and D.NOLO are among the highlights.

France and the 50th

Bifurcating the boundary between Edina and Minneapolis, 50th and France is a charming retail area renowned for its high-end shops, niche retailers, and top-notch eating choices. There are several distinctive stores in the region, giving it the charm of a little town.

Downtown Minneapolis' Nicollet Mall Nicollet Mall is a pedestrian-friendly shopping center with a variety of eateries, specialty shops, and department stores. Remarkable destinations, including Macy's, Saks Off 5th, and the IDS Center, may be found in this key retail area.

Lyn-Lake

Vintage shops, independent boutiques, and art galleries may be found among the varied selection of businesses in Lyn-Lake, which is focused around the junction of Lyndale Avenue and Lake Street. There is a thriving arts and cultural scene in this neighborhood.

Farmers Markets and Craft Fairs

Farmers Market in Minneapolis

The Minneapolis Farmers Market, one of the biggest and most well-liked farmers markets in the city, is open all year round and offers a variety of fresh fruit, meats, cheeses, and handcrafted crafts. Situated on Lyndale Avenue, it's a neighborhood mainstay for locally sourced and fresh goods.

Farmers Market in Mill City

This farmers market, which is held in the historic Mill City Museum neighborhood, focuses on organic, sustainable, and locally produced goods. It is open on Saturdays from May through October and provides a wide variety of products, such as baked foods, meats, fresh fruit, and handcrafted items.

Minneapolis Farmers Market in the Northeast

Nestled in the Northeast Arts District, this market is a community hub renowned for its fine local products and welcoming environment. From May through October, it is open on Saturdays and features live entertainment, handcrafted goods, and fresh cuisine.

Farmers Market in Fulton

The Fulton Farmers Market, a neighborhood mainstay with a wide selection of locally grown fruit, meats, and prepared dishes, is located in South Minneapolis. Open from May through October, it's the ideal place to purchase locally sourced and fresh goods.

Farmers Market in Midtown

The Midtown Farmers Market, which is situated at the junction of Lake Street and Hiawatha Avenue, sells regional crafts, meats, and fruit. It offers a lively shopping experience and is open on Saturdays from May through October as well as Tuesdays from June through October.

Craft Market in Minneapolis

Pop-up events highlighting local makers and artists are held across the city by the Minneapolis Craft Market. You may discover some amazing handcrafted items there, such as apparel, jewelry, and artwork. There are events all year-round at different venues.

Powderhorn Art Fair

The Powderhorn Art Fair, an annual event held in August in Powderhorn Park, features the creations of hundreds of regional and national artists. Offering a large selection of handcrafted items, crafts, and artwork, it's a significant event in the local art scene.

Uptown Art Fair

One of the biggest outdoor art events in the Midwest is the Uptown Art Fair, which happens in early August. More than 350 artists' pieces, live music, food vendors, and interactive art activities are all included.

Synopsis

Minneapolis has a diverse range of shopping experiences, including lively farmers markets and artisan fairs, exclusive shops, and busy retail areas. There is something for every kind of consumer, from fresh vegetables and handcrafted crafts at local markets to stylish apparel and home items in Uptown and the North Loop. Every market and neighborhood has a distinct vibe that highlights the city's inventive and varied personality.

CHAPTER TEN: CONCLUSION

Recap of Highlights

1. Cultural Landmarks: Minneapolis Institute of Art: This institution has over 90,000 pieces of art spanning 5,000 years, including Native American, Asian, and African works.

Walker Art Center and Minneapolis Sculpture Garden: Contains famous sculptures, including the Spoonbridge and Cherry, as well as modern art shows.

2. Parks and Nature: Chain of Lakes: Lake Harriet, Lake Calhoun (Bde Maka Ska), and Lake of the Isles. Biking, walking, and boating facilities are available.

Minnehaha Park is well-known for its gorgeous walking paths and the 53-foot-tall Minnehaha Falls.

Regional Park Theodore Wirth provides a variety of sports, such as cross-country skiing and golf.

3. Historical Sites: Mill City Museum: Contains exhibits housed within a historic mill building, chronicling the flour milling industry that drove the city's expansion.

Fort Snelling: An old military fort that provides information on the Dakota people and early Minnesota history.

4. City Touring: North Loop: A hip district includes fine dining options, boutique stores, and an exciting nightlife.

Nicollet Mall: A downtown pedestrian-friendly avenue including eateries, retail establishments, and public artwork.

5. Cultural Scene: Well-known for its wide range of culinary options, which include international cuisine, farm-to-table restaurants, and signature local dishes like the Juicy Lucy burger. Notable locations include Matt's Bar for Juicy Lucy, Hell's Kitchen for inventive brunches, and The Bachelor Farmer for food with a Scandinavian flair.

6. Music and Performing Arts: First Avenue: Prince made this iconic music venue renowned.

Guthrie Theater: Featuring magnificent views of the Mississippi River, this theater presents top-notch theatrical shows.

Tips for a Memorable Trip

1. Plan Seasonally: There are several seasons in Minneapolis. Winter has winter sports and holiday celebrations, while summer provides fantastic outdoor activities. The pleasant weather in the spring and autumn makes them ideal for city exploration.

2. Transportation: Take advantage of the buses and light rail systems of the Metro Transit system. Think about riding; Minneapolis has many bike paths and rental companies like Nice Ride.

3. Stay Uptown or Downtown: These neighborhoods provide quick access to popular sights, restaurants, and nightlife. For something more individualized, think about vacation rentals or boutique hotels.

4. Dining Reservations: To prevent lengthy waits, book reservations in advance for popular restaurants, particularly those in the North Loop or Uptown.

5. Outdoor Gear: Wear layers, boots, and warm accessories like hats and gloves if you're coming in the winter. Sunglasses, sunscreen, and comfy walking shoes are musts in the summer.

6. Local Events: Look for celebrations, performances, and festivals in your area. Events like the Minneapolis Aquatennial take place in the summer, while Holidazzle is celebrated in the winter.

7. Safety: Although you should be safe in general, pay attention to your surroundings, particularly at night. Remain in crowded, well-lit locations.

8. Cultural Etiquette: Show consideration for the history and culture of the area, especially with respect to historic places and indigenous heritage.

9. Budgeting: Minneapolis has a lot to offer in terms of activities, from fine restaurants to free parks and galleries. Budget your money so that you may enjoy both free and expensive sights and memorable experiences.

10. Local Insights: Ask others who live there for suggestions. They may provide insightful information on hidden treasures and the ideal times to explore well-known locations.

Final Thoughts and Farewell

Minneapolis provides a distinctive mix of urban and outdoor experiences because of its rich history, dynamic cultural environment, and stunning natural surroundings. Every part of the city has something to offer, from the peaceful trails along the Chain of Lakes to the busy streets of downtown. Regardless of your interests—fine art, history, cuisine, or outdoor exploration—Minneapolis extends a warm welcome and a wealth of opportunities to make lifelong memories.

Don't forget to enjoy the many gastronomic options, immerse yourself in the local culture, and explore the city's many parks and trails. Every trip to

Minneapolis may bring with it fresh experiences and treasured memories.

Consider the highlights and unusual situations that contributed to the great moments of your vacation as you are ready to depart. Keep these memories in mind and think about coming back to see more of what Minneapolis has to offer.

HAPPY TRAVELS!!!

Printed in Great Britain
by Amazon

52900044R00073